Fabulous Cookies

by Marie Bianco

BARRON'S

Woodbury, New York • London • Toronto • Sydney

All inquiries should be addressed to:

Barron's Educational Series, Inc.
113 Crossways Park Drive
Woodbury, New York 11797

International Standard Book
No. 0-8120-5528-4
Library of Congress Catalog Card
No. 83-9945

**Library of Congress Cataloging
in Publication Data**
Bianco, Marie.
  fabulous cookies.

  (Barron's easy cooking series)
  Includes index.
  1. Cookies. I. Title. II. Title:
fabulous cookies. III. Series.
TX772.B55 1983   641.8′654   83-9945
ISBN 0-8120-5528-4

PRINTED IN THE
UNITED STATES OF AMERICA
4 5 6   880   9 8 7 6 5 4

Credits

Photography
Color photographs: Irwin Horowitz
Food preparation: Andrea Swenson
Stylist: Hal Walter

Author Marie Bianco is a food writer for a
  Long Island newspaper

Cover and book design Milton Glaser, Inc.

Series editor Carole Berglie

INTRODUCTION

Cookies and small cakes are fun to make and fun to eat. Moreover, they are a wonderful introduction to the world of baking. Some of the recipes here need no introduction; others are variations on a theme. All are delicious and easy to make.

Cookies are made from the same basic ingredients—flour, sugar, a few eggs, flavoring, and perhaps nuts or chocolate. Also included are a few easy-to-make cakes.

Before getting started, here are some of the essentials you will need to know.

Read all the directions first.

Unless a specific flour is called for, use all-purpose flour in all these recipes. It is unnecessary to sift flour if it is labeled "presifted."

Use butter whenever possible for a better flavor. Margarine can be substituted but the taste will not be as delicate.

Nuts are usually interchangeable. Walnuts can be used instead of pecans and almonds or vice versa. To chop nuts with a food processor use an on/off motion. Too much of their natural oils will be extracted if the machine is left on too long.

For more nutrition in cookies and cakes, it is possible to substitute whole-wheat flour for half the amount of all-purpose flour. This will, however, change the texture and taste of the cookie.

Before baking, take out all the ingredients first and place them within easy reach. Clean up can be done while the goodies are in the oven.

For measuring dry ingredients such as flour and sugar, use stacked 1, ½, ⅓ and ¼ cups. Spoon in the ingredient and level off with the flat edge of a knife. Liquid ingredients should be poured into a glass measuring cup and placed on a level surface at eye level.

Preheat oven for at least 15 minutes before baking.

All these recipes call for large eggs.

To chill cookie dough, wrap securely in plastic wrap and refrigerate. To hasten the process, you can put it into the freezer.

A cookie sheet is a flat piece of metal with a lip only on one side. Pans with edges reflect heat and tend to over-cook the cookies around the edges. A pan with sides also makes them more difficult to remove.

Some cookies require an ungreased pan, so don't grease it unless instructed. Unsalted butter, margarine, or solid vegetable shortening work best. Use a small piece of wax paper to spread the fat around. If instructed to dust with flour, sprinkle with about 2 tablespoons of flour and tap out any excess over the sink.

All recipes here can be made with a mixer, if available. Use low speed to mix ingredients, medium speed to cream butter and sugar. Butter should be at room temperature or it will not blend smoothly with the sugar. To mix by hand, use a wooden spoon. Do not over beat; this tends to make baked goods tough.

Allow plenty of room for unbaked cookies to spread. The more butter they contain, the more they usually spread. Those placed too near the edge will brown unevenly.

If using 1 cookie sheet, place it in the center of the oven. When using 2, place racks to divide oven in thirds. Place one sheet on the upper rack and one on the lower rack.

Half way during the baking time, reverse pans front to back, and also reverse their positions, placing the top one on the bottom and the bottom one on top.

For cakes, place a single pan in the center of the oven. For 2 layers, place them at opposite ends of the oven and then reverse them half way through the baking time for more even cooking.

A good oven thermometer is a necessity for a baker. It only costs a few dollars and the correct temperature ensures a better product.

When using the sheets for a second batch of cookies, make sure the pans have cooled first.

Never bake more than 2 cookie sheets at a time.

To have all cookies, such as drop or molded cookies, come out to the same size, measure the dough with a measuring spoon or spoon the dough onto a sheet of wax paper and "eye-ball" them for size.

Roll out cookies using a canvas pastry cloth and a covered rolling pin with as little extra flour as possible. When rolling out cookies, cut them as close to each other as possible and then re-roll scraps. Too much re-rolling tends to produce tough cookies.

For proper circulation, the baking pans should be 2 inches shorter than the width and depth of the oven.

When minimum baking time is up, check for doneness. The shorter time will give you a softer cookie, the longer time will produce a crisp cookie. Left on the baking sheet, cookies will continue to cook.

Store crisp and soft cookies in separate containers. Soft ones should be kept in containers with loose-fitting lids; a slice of apple will keep the cookies soft, but should be replaced regularly. Crisp cookies can be stored in coffee or shortening cans or other containers that close tightly. To restore crispness, heat them in a 300-degree oven for 5 minutes. Bar cookies can be stored right in their baking pans covered with aluminum foil or plastic wrap.

To test for doneness, check that thin cookies are firm to the touch and slightly browned around the edges. Drop cookies should leave no imprint when tapped in the center. Bar cookies are done when they pull away from the sides of the pan. Cakes are done when a cake tester or a toothpick comes out clean when inserted in the center.

To transfer cookies after baking, use a broad spatula. Since there never seem to be enough racks available when baking a large amount of cookies, cool them on wax paper on a flat surface. Never stack warm cookies on each other; they will not be flat and may stick to each other.

Cookies can be frozen after baking at 0 degrees for up to 6 months. To freeze them, lay them on a flat surface and when they are frozen, pack them in containers with rigid sides using wax paper between layers. Baked cookies take only about 5 minutes to defrost. Uncooked cookie dough can be frozen if wrapped securely in plastic wrap. Defrost the dough at room temperature for about 30 to 40 minutes before baking.

When mailing cookies choose only those that are up to traveling, such as bar cookies or drop cookies. Wrap each one separately in foil or plastic wrap and place them in a sturdy cardboard box. Fill in any corners of the box with crushed wax paper and mark box "fragile." Make sure someone will be there when they are delivered.

Decorated cookies can be a three-day affair. Make the dough one day, bake them the next and decorate them on the third day.

UNDERSTANDING THE
RECIPE ANALYSES

For each recipe, you'll note that we have provided data on the quantities of protein, fat, sodium, carbohydrates, and potassium, as well as the number of calories (kcal) per serving or per cookie. The calculations are fundamentally estimates, and should be followed only in a very general way. The actual quantities of substances will vary if you make your cookies larger or smaller than suggested or if you make substitutions of ingredients. If you must watch your diet closely, we suggest you consult your physician.

YIELD

3 dozen

Per cookie
calories 133, protein 2 g,
fat 7 g, sodium 116 mg,
carbohydrates 16 g, potassium
94 mg

TIME

10 minutes preparation
12 to 15 minutes baking

INGREDIENTS

I cup butter, softened
I cup firmly packed brown sugar
I cup puréed pumpkin
I egg
I teaspoon vanilla extract
2 cups all-purpose flour
I teaspoon baking powder
½ teaspoon baking soda
½ teaspoon salt

I teaspoon ground cinnamon
½ teaspoon ground nutmeg
¼ teaspoon ground allspice
I cup raisins
I cup chopped walnuts

Preheat the oven to 350 degrees. Lightly grease a cookie sheet.

In a medium bowl cream the butter and sugar ①. Add the pumpkin, egg, and vanilla. Beat well.

In a separate bowl combine the flour, baking powder, baking soda, salt, cinnamon, nutmeg, and allspice. Add to the creamed mixture and blend well ②. Stir in the raisins and walnuts ③.

Drop mixture by rounded tablespoons onto the cookie sheet, about 2 inches apart. Bake for 12 to 15 minutes, or until cookie springs back when depressed with a finger. Remove and cool.

YIELD

32 bars

Per cookie
calories 135, protein 2 g,
fat 4 g, sodium 57 mg,
carbohydrates 26 g, potassium
118 mg

TIME

30 minutes preparation
20 minutes chilling
15 to 18 minutes baking

INGREDIENTS

1¼ cups whole-wheat flour
1¼ cups all-purpose flour
¼ teaspoon baking soda
¼ teaspoon salt
½ cup butter, softened
1 cup granulated sugar
2 eggs
1 teaspoon vanilla extract

FILLING

1 pound dried figs
⅓ cup granulated sugar
½ cup water
1 teaspoon grated lemon rind

In a large bowl combine the whole-wheat and all-purpose flours. Stir in the baking soda and salt.

Cream the butter and sugar until light and fluffy. Add the eggs and vanilla and mix well. Add the dry ingredients and stir until well blended. Chill while making the filling.

Chop the figs in a meat grinder or food processor. Add the sugar, water, and lemon rind. Place in a medium saucepan and simmer for 5 minutes to thicken. Cool. Lightly grease a cookie sheet.

On a lightly floured surface or between 2 sheets of wax paper, roll out half the dough into an 8 by 16-inch rectangle. Cut lengthwise into 2 strips, each 4 by 16 inches. Place one quarter of the fig mixture evenly down the center of each strip ①. Fold the sides of the dough over the filling and press edges lightly ②.

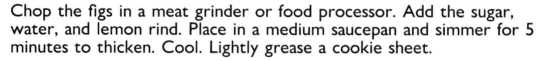

Flip the strips over with a broad spatula and cut in half ③. Transfer to the cookie sheet and chill for 20 minutes.

Preheat the oven to 375 degrees.

Bake cookies for 15 to 18 minutes or until lightly browned. Cut into 2-inch lengths while still warm using a sharp knife, then cool.

YIELD

3 dozen

Per cookie
calories 97, protein 1 g, fat 6 g, sodium 30 mg, carbohydrates 10 g, potassium 49 mg

TIME

30 minutes preparation
8 to 10 minutes baking

INGREDIENTS

⅔ cup granulated sugar
½ cup butter
2 tablespoons light corn syrup
2 tablespoons milk
1 cup sliced almonds
½ cup all-purpose flour
2 tablespoons finely chopped candied cherries
2 tablespoons finely minced citron or orange rind
½ teaspoon vanilla extract
1 cup semisweet chocolate morsels

Preheat the oven to 350 degrees. Cover a cookie sheet with aluminum foil, then lightly butter and flour the sheet.

In a medium saucepan combine the sugar, butter, corn syrup, and milk. Over medium heat cook to 232 degrees on a candy thermometer (soft ball stage).

Remove from the heat and stir in almonds, flour, candied fruits, and vanilla. Mix well. Drop by teaspoonfuls onto the cookie sheet ①, allowing about 4 inches of space between the cookies. Bake for 8 to 10 minutes, or until brown around the edges. Peel cookies off foil and cool completely.

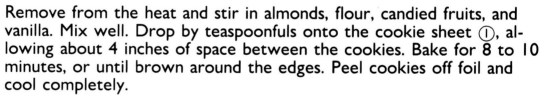

Heat the chocolate chips over hot (*not* boiling) water until melted. Spread the bottom side of each cookie with melted chocolate ② and place on a wire rack to harden ③. If desired, draw a decorating comb or other clean comb over the chocolate to form swirls.

NOTE Do not attempt to make these cookies on an exceptionally damp day. They will remain sticky when removed from oven.

GINGERBREAD PEOPLE

YIELD

2 dozen, about 5 inches high

Per cookie
calories 144, protein 2 g, fat 4 g, sodium 117 mg, carbohydrates 26 g, potassium 219 mg

TIME

20 minutes preparation
2 to 3 hours chilling
8 to 10 minutes baking

INGREDIENTS

½ cup butter, softened
½ cup granulated sugar
½ cup molasses
1 egg yolk
2 cups all-purpose flour
½ teaspoon salt
1 teaspoon baking powder
½ teaspoon baking soda
1½ teaspoons ground cinnamon
1 teaspoon ground cloves

1 teaspoon ground ginger
½ teaspoon ground nutmeg

ICING

2¼ cups sifted confectioners' sugar
2 egg whites
¼ teaspoon cream of tartar

In a large bowl cream together the butter, sugar, and molasses. Add the egg yolk and mix well.

Sift together the flour, salt, baking powder, baking soda, cinnamon, cloves, ginger, and nutmeg. Stir into the molasses mixture and mix well. Chill for 2 to 3 hours.

Preheat the oven to 350 degrees.

On a lightly floured surface roll out the dough until it is ¼ inch thick ①. Cut with gingerbread boy and girl cutters ②. Place cookies on an ungreased cookie sheet and bake for 8 to 10 minutes or until cookies spring back when depressed slightly. Cool on a rack.

With an electric mixer at high speed beat together the confectioners' sugar, egg whites, and cream of tartar until the icing holds a peak ③. Fill a decorating tube or pastry bag. Outline the cookies and mark the eyes and mouths. Allow icing to set before serving cookies or storing them.

FOUR-LAYERED PINEAPPLE STRIPS

YIELD

18 small pastries

Per pastry
calories 123, protein 2 g,
fat 6 g, sodium 121 mg,
carbohydrates 16 g, potassium
38 mg

TIME

20 minutes preparation
30 minutes chilling
45 minutes baking

INGREDIENTS

1 can (8¼ ounces) crushed pineapple, drained (reserve syrup)
1 tablespoon cornstarch
⅓ cup plus 2 tablespoons granulated sugar
Dash of mace
½ cup butter
1 egg, separated
½ teaspoon vanilla extract
¼ teaspoon almond extract

1½ cups all-purpose flour
½ teaspoon salt
¼ teaspoon baking powder
2 tablespoons sliced almonds

In a small saucepan combine the crushed pineapple, cornstarch, 2 tablespoons of sugar, and mace. Cook, stirring constantly, until the mixture boils and thickens. Remove from heat and cool.

Cream the butter, remaining sugar, egg yolk, and vanilla and almond extracts. Sift the flour with the salt and baking powder and blend into the butter mixture, alternating with 1½ tablespoons of the reserved pineapple syrup. Cover and chill for 30 minutes.

Preheat the oven to 325 degrees.

Divide the batter into 2 equal portions and shape each into a rectangle. Roll each rectangle to 7 by 11 inches between 2 sheets of wax paper. Spread half the pineapple filling down the center of each rectangle ①, covering the center third of the dough. Use spatulas to lift each edge of the dough, then fold the lengthwise sides over the filling ②, leaving about ¾ inch space between the 2 sides.

Beat the egg white lightly, then brush it over the dough. Fold again in half lengthwise ③, so the pastry makes a narrow 4-layered strip. Brush the tops with egg white, and sprinkle each strip with a tablespoon of almonds. Lift pastries onto a baking sheet using broad spatulas. Bake for 45 minutes, until lightly browned. Cool for 10 minutes on the baking sheet, then slide carefully onto a wire rack to cool completely. When cold, cut diagonally into strips about 1¼ inches wide.

FORGOTTEN MERINGUES

YIELD

2 dozen

Per cookie
calories 26, protein .5 g,
fat .5 g, sodium 29 mg,
carbohydrates 5 g, potassium
11 mg

TIME

20 minutes preparation
1 hour or overnight
    baking

INGREDIENTS

3 egg whites, at room temperature
1/4 teaspoon salt
1/4 teaspoon cream of tartar
1/2 cup granulated sugar
1/2 teaspoon almond extract
1/2 cup dessicated coconut or finely
    chopped pecans

Preheat the oven to 200 degrees. Line a cookie sheet with brown paper or kitchen parchment.

In a large, greasefree mixing bowl beat the egg whites until frothy. Add the salt and cream of tartar and beat well. Slowly add the sugar, a tablespoon at a time, until the mixture is shiny and holds a firm tip when the beater is lifted ①. Gently fold in the almond extract and coconut or pecans ②.

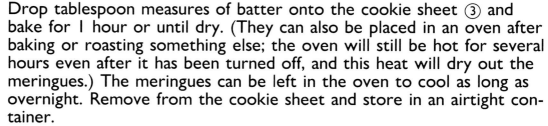

Drop tablespoon measures of batter onto the cookie sheet ③ and bake for 1 hour or until dry. (They can also be placed in an oven after baking or roasting something else; the oven will still be hot for several hours even after it has been turned off, and this heat will dry out the meringues.) The meringues can be left in the oven to cool as long as overnight. Remove from the cookie sheet and store in an airtight container.

NOTE *If desired, sprinkle coconut meringues with toasted coconut just before baking.*

CHOCOLATE SANDWICH COOKIES

YIELD

3 dozen

Per cookie

calories 110, protein 1 g, fat 4 g, sodium 61 mg, carbohydrates 18 g, potassium 28 mg

TIME

15 minutes preparation
3 to 4 hours chilling
8 to 10 minutes baking

INGREDIENTS

½ cup butter, softened
1 cup granulated sugar
1 egg
1 teaspoon vanilla extract
1¼ cups all-purpose flour
½ cup cocoa
¾ teaspoon baking soda
¼ teaspoon salt

CREAMY FILLING

¼ cup butter, softened
2½ cups sifted confectioners' sugar
1 teaspoon vanilla extract
2 tablespoons milk

In a medium bowl cream the butter, sugar, egg, and vanilla.

Sift together the flour, cocoa, baking soda, and salt; add to sugar mixture.

Shape the dough into two 1½-inch-thick rolls. Wrap in plastic wrap and chill for 3 to 4 hours.

Preheat the oven to 375 degrees.

Cut each dough roll into ⅛-inch slices. Place slices on an ungreased cookie sheet. Decorate slices by drawing the tines of a fork across each slice ①. Bake cookies for 8 to 10 minutes or until almost firm.

To make the filling, combine all ingredients in a small bowl and beat until spreading consistency. Spread half the cookies with the filling ②; top each with a plain half ③.

CRANBERRY MUFFINS

YIELD

12

Per serving
calories 187, protein 3 g,
fat 8 g, sodium 123 mg,
carbohydrates 26 g, potassium
81 mg

TIME

15 minutes preparation
20 minutes baking

INGREDIENTS

2¼ cups all-purpose flour
¾ cup granulated sugar
1 teaspoon baking soda
¼ teaspoon salt
1 egg, slightly beaten
1¼ cups buttermilk
4 tablespoons butter, melted
1 cup chopped cranberries
½ cup chopped pecans or walnuts
Confectioners' sugar

Preheat the oven to 400 degrees. Lightly grease a muffin tin or fill cupcake tins with paper liners.

In a large bowl combine the flour, ¼ cup sugar, baking soda, and salt. Toss lightly with a fork ①.

In a small bowl, combine the egg, buttermilk, and butter and blend well. Add to the dry ingredients and stir just enough to moisten ②.

Toss the cranberries with the remaining sugar and add to the batter, along with the chopped nuts. Spoon batter into the muffin or cupcake tins, filling them two-thirds full ③. Bake for 20 minutes, or until a cake tester comes out clean. Sprinkle with confectioners' sugar and serve warm.

LORETTA'S CHOCOLATE-CHIP MANDEL BREAD

YIELD

2 dozen slices

Per slice

calories 252, protein 3 g,
fat 16 g, sodium 27 mg,
carbohydrates 26 g, potassium
88 mg

TIME

15 minutes preparation
20 to 25 minutes baking

INGREDIENTS

3 cups all-purpose flour
1 teaspoon baking powder
3 eggs, beaten
1 cup granulated sugar
1 cup vegetable oil
1 teaspoon almond extract
1 cup semisweet chocolate morsels
1 cup chopped almonds
Cinnamon and granulated sugar

Preheat the oven to 375 degrees. Grease 2 cookie sheets.

Combine the flour and baking powder. Mix eggs, sugar, oil, and almond extract and add to the dry ingredients. Add the chocolate morsels and the nuts. This dough will be very thick, but blend ingredients well.

Divide the dough into 2 portions. Place each half on a cookie sheet, stretching and patting it into a long rectangle about 13 by 4 inches ①. (It helps to moisten your hands with oil.) Sprinkle the tops of the dough with cinnamon and sugar ②. Bake for 20 to 25 minutes or until the cake springs back when pressed in the center. Cool.

Slice the cakes on the diagonal ③ and lay the pieces on their side. Carefully brown under the broiler.

YIELD

3 to 4 dozen

Per cookie

calories 141, protein 2 g,
fat 9 g, sodium 55 mg,
carbohydrates 14 g, potassium
48 mg

TIME

15 minutes preparation
7 to 10 minutes baking

INGREDIENTS

1 cup butter, softened
½ cup granulated sugar
1 teaspoon vanilla extract
2⅓ cups all-purpose flour
¾ cup finely chopped nuts
36 to 48 milk chocolate Kisses
Confectioners' sugar

Preheat the oven to 375 degrees.

Cream the butter, sugar, and vanilla in a large mixer bowl until light and fluffy ①. Add the flour and chopped nuts; blend well.

Remove the foil from the candies.

Shape about 1 tablespoon of dough around each candy ②, covering it completely. Place on an ungreased cookie sheet and bake for 7 to 10 minutes or until set but not brown.

Cool; roll in confectioners' sugar ③, and store in an airtight container. Roll in sugar again before serving.

GINNY'S RUGALAH

YIELD

*4 dozen large or 8 dozen
   small*

Per pastry (48)
*calories 79, protein 1 g,
fat 5 g, sodium 54 mg,
carbohydrates 8 g,
potassium 31 mg*

TIME

*30 minutes preparation
Overnight chilling
18 to 20 minutes baking*

INGREDIENTS

*8 ounces cottage cheese
³/₄ cup plus 2 tablespoons butter
2 cups all-purpose flour*

FILLING

*³/₄ cup finely chopped walnuts
³/₄ cup firmly packed light brown
   sugar
³/₄ teaspoon cinnamon*

In a medium bowl, combine the cottage cheese with ½ cup butter. Cream until soft, then add the flour and mix well. Wrap the dough in plastic wrap and chill overnight.

Preheat the oven to 400 degrees. Lightly grease a cookie sheet.

Make the filling by combining the walnuts, brown sugar, and cinnamon. Roll out the dough, a third at a time, on a lightly floured surface until it is ⅛ inch thick. Using a ruler and a sharp knife, mark the dough into strips ①, 1 by 4 inches for small pastries and 1 by 8 inches for large ones.

Melt the remaining butter, and brush the dough with the butter ②. Sprinkle with the nut mixture, then roll up pastries and place seam side down on the cookie sheet ③. Brush tops with any remaining butter.

Bake pastries in oven for 18 to 20 minutes, or until they are light brown. Cool and serve.

BETSY'S KRINGLER CAKES

YIELD

8 to 12 servings

Per serving
calories 148, protein 2 g,
fat 10 g, sodium 88 mg,
carbohydrates 14 g, potassium
35 mg

TIME

20 minutes preparation
45 to 55 minutes baking

INGREDIENTS

2 cups all-purpose flour
1 cup butter, cut in chunks
1 cup plus 2 tablespoons cold water
3 eggs
1/2 teaspoon almond extract

ICING

1 cup sifted confectioners' sugar
1 teaspoon butter, softened
1/2 teaspoon almond extract
2 to 3 teaspoons milk
1/3 cup sliced almonds

Preheat the oven to 375 degrees.

Place half the flour in a medium bowl and cut in half the butter, using a pastry blender, 2 knives, or your fingertips ①. Add the 2 tablespoons of water, a tablespoon at a time, stirring constantly. Gather the mixture into a ball ②, divide in half, then press each half into a 12-by-3-inch rectangle on an ungreased cookie sheet ③. Set aside.

In a medium saucepan bring the 1 cup of water and the remaining butter to a boil. Simmer until the butter melts, then remove from the heat and add the remaining flour all at once. Beat until smooth and the mixture begins to form a ball. Add the eggs, 1 at a time, stirring well after each addition. Add the almond extract and blend. Spread this mixture evenly over the dough on the cookie sheet and bake for 45 to 55 minutes until golden brown. Cool.

Combine the confectioners' sugar for the icing with the butter and almond extract. Add the milk, 1 teaspoon at a time, until mixture is spreading consistency. Spread over the cooled pastry, then sprinkle with sliced almonds and press them down slightly. When icing is set, serve, cutting into strips or slices.

YIELD

5 to 6 dozen

Per cookie (5 dozen)
calories 81, protein 1 g, fat 5 g, sodium 60 mg, carbohydrates 11 g, potassium 14 mg

TIME

10 to 15 minutes
    preparation
2 to 3 hours chilling
10 to 12 minutes baking

INGREDIENTS

4 cups all-purpose flour
1 teaspoon baking powder
½ teaspoon baking soda
½ teaspoon salt
½ teaspoon ground nutmeg
1 tablespoon grated lemon rind
1 cup butter, softened
1¼ cups granulated sugar
1 egg
¾ cup sour cream
1 teaspoon vanilla extract

In a medium bowl combine the flour, baking powder, baking soda, salt, nutmeg, and lemon rind. Toss lightly with a fork to mix.

In a large bowl cream the butter and sugar until light and fluffy. Add the egg, sour cream, and vanilla and combine well. Add the flour mixture to the creamed mixture and mix well. Refrigerate 2 to 3 hours.

Preheat the oven to 375 degrees. Lightly grease a cookie sheet.

Roll out one quarter of the dough at a time onto a lightly floured surface. Roll until ¼ inch thick, then cut with floured cookie cutters ①. Roll and cut remaining dough. Reroll and cut scraps. Transfer cookies to the cookie sheet using a broad spatula, and bake for 10 to 12 minutes, or until cookies are lightly browned. Cool completely on a rack.

VARIATIONS Brush the uncooked cookies with slightly beaten egg white ② and sprinkle with colored sugar, sprinkles, or jimmies ③. Or place a walnut or pecan half in the center of each cookie before baking.

CHOCOLATE CHEWY CRITTERS

YIELD

2½ dozen

Per cookie
calories 125, protein 1 g,
fat 7 g, sodium 48 mg,
carbohydrates 15 g, potassium
60 mg

TIME

20 minutes preparation
12 to 14 minutes baking

INGREDIENTS

½ cup firmly packed light brown
   sugar
½ cup butter, softened
2 tablespoons milk
½ teaspoon vanilla extract
1½ cups all-purpose flour
¼ teaspoon salt
Approximately 120 pecan halves
15 vanilla caramels, cut in half
   lengthwise
1 cup semisweet chocolate morsels

Preheat the oven to 350 degrees.

Cream the sugar and butter. Add the milk and vanilla, then stir in the flour and salt.

On an ungreased cookie sheet arrange 4 pecan halves at right angles to one another ①. Divide the dough into 30 equal portions. Form each piece of dough around a piece of caramel ②, covering the candy completely. Press each one firmly on a cluster of pecan halves ③. Bake for 12 to 14 minutes or until firm. Cool completely on a rack.

Over hot (*not* boiling) water, melt the chocolate. Brush each cookie with chocolate, but do not cover nuts. Refrigerate until set.

YIELD

18 giant cookies

Per cookie

calories 325, protein 3 g,
fat 18 g, sodium 105 mg,
carbohydrates 40 g, potassium
119 mg

TIME

10 minutes preparation
12 to 14 minutes baking

INGREDIENTS

¾ cup granulated sugar
¾ cup firmly packed brown sugar
½ cup butter, softened
½ cup vegetable shortening
2 eggs
1 teaspoon vanilla extract
2¼ cups all-purpose flour
1 teaspoon baking soda

1 teaspoon cream of tartar
¼ teaspoon salt
12 ounces (2 cups) semisweet
   chocolate morsels
Granulated sugar

Preheat the oven to 350 degrees. Lightly grease a cookie sheet.

In a mixing bowl cream the sugars with the butter and shortening until light and fluffy. Add the eggs 1 at a time, beating well after each addition. Stir in vanilla.

Sift together the flour, baking soda, cream of tartar, and salt and add to the sugar mixture, beating well. Fold in the chocolate chips.

Form ¼ cup of batter into a ball ① and roll it in the granulated sugar ②. Place on the cookie sheet and, with the fingertips, press into a 4-inch circle ③. Bake for 12 to 14 minutes, or until cookie springs back when pressed on top. Cool on sheet for 1 minute before removing to a rack to cool completely.

CHILD'S BIRTHDAY CAKE

YIELD

12 servings

Per cookie
calories 463, protein 5 g,
fat 16 g, sodium 314 mg,
carbohydrates 76 g, potassium
125 mg

TIME

1 hour preparation
30 minutes baking

INGREDIENTS

3 cups sifted cake flour
2½ teaspoons baking powder
½ teaspoon salt
⅔ cup butter
1½ cups granulated sugar
2 eggs
1 teaspoon vanilla extract
1¼ cups milk

ICING

2 egg whites
1½ cups granulated sugar
¼ teaspoon cream of tartar
⅓ cup water
1 teaspoon vanilla extract

DECORATION

2 cups dessicated coconut
Food coloring
Jelly beans

Preheat the oven to 350 degrees. Lightly grease and then line with wax paper or parchment paper 2 cake pans, one a 9-inch square and the other an 8-inch round pan.

Sift together the flour, baking powder, and salt. In a large bowl, cream the butter, then add the sugar and continue to cream until mixture is light and fluffy. Add the eggs, 1 at a time, mixing well after each. Stir in the vanilla. Add the dry mixture to the creamed mixture, alternating with the milk and starting and ending with the dry mix.

Divide batter between the 2 cake pans and bake for 30 minutes or until a cake tester comes out clean. Cool on racks for 10 minutes, then remove from pans ①, peel off paper, and cool completely.

Make the icing in the top of a double boiler by combining the egg whites, sugar, cream of tartar, and water. Beat with a hand electric mixer for 1 minute, then place over hot water and cook for 7 minutes, beating constantly until the mixture is soft and glossy. Remove from the heat and add the vanilla.

Cut the square cake into a t-shape and remove the rectangular pieces on either side ②. Cut these in half crosswise and attach each strip onto the cross pieces of the t to make legs. Use the round cake for the head.

Divide the coconut into 4 small dessert dishes. Leave 1 dish uncolored and tint the others yellow, red, and blue. Pat the coconut onto the cake: yellow for the hair, blue and red for the shirt and pants, and white for the face, arms, and legs ③. Fill in the facial features with jelly beans.

YIELD

1½ to 2 dozen
Per cookie (18)
calories 248, protein 4 g,
fat 13 g, sodium 234 mg,
carbohydrates 31 g, potassium
225 mg

TIME

10 minutes preparation
15 minutes baking

INGREDIENTS

¾ cup butter, softened
1¼ cups firmly packed brown sugar
1 egg
¼ cup frozen orange juice
   concentrate
1 cup whole-wheat flour
¼ cup nonfat dry milk
1 teaspoon salt
1 teaspoon baking powder

¼ teaspoon ground cinnamon
¼ cup wheat germ
1 cup chopped walnuts
1½ cups quick-cooking rolled oats
½ cup raisins
Granulated sugar
Additional chopped and halved
   walnuts for decoration

Preheat the oven to 350 degrees. Lightly grease a cookie sheet.

Cream together the butter, brown sugar, and egg until fluffy. Add the orange juice concentrate and blend.

Mix together the flour, nonfat dry milk, salt, baking powder, cinnamon, and wheat germ. Add the creamed mixture and stir well. Stir in chopped walnuts, rolled oats, and raisins.

Drop batter by heaping tablespoonfuls onto the baking sheet ①. Flatten heaps to about 3¼ inches wide with the bottom of a glass dipped in sugar ②. Sprinkle each cookie with a few additional walnuts ③ and top with walnut halve.

Bake for 15 minutes or until cookie springs back when pressed on top. Let stand 2 to 3 minutes, then lift off with a broad spatula to cool on a wire rack.

YIELD

16 bars

Per cookie
calories 154, protein 2 g,
fat 8 g, sodium 71 mg,
carbohydrates 19 g, potassium
93 mg

TIME

10 minutes preparation
25 minutes baking

INGREDIENTS

1/4 cup butter
1 cup firmly packed light brown sugar
1 egg
3/4 cup all-purpose flour
1 teaspoon baking powder
Dash of salt
1 teaspoon vanilla extract
1 cup chopped walnuts

Preheat the oven to 350 degrees. Generously grease an 8-inch square baking pan.

Melt the butter and add the brown sugar. Cook, stirring constantly, for 30 seconds or until well blended. Cool, then add the egg.

Combine the flour, baking powder, and salt and add to the brown sugar mixture ①. Stir in the vanilla and walnuts, then spread in the baking pan ②. Bake for 25 minutes, or until a toothpick inserted in the center comes out clean ③. Cool and cut into squares.

CHERRY BON-BONS

YIELD

2½ dozen

Per cookie
calories 148, protein 3 g,
fat 7 g, sodium 70 mg,
carbohydrates 18 g,
potassium 27 mg

TIME

20 minutes preparation
30 to 45 minutes baking

INGREDIENTS

¾ cup butter, softened
¾ cup granulated sugar
½ teaspoon vanilla extract
¼ teaspoon salt
1¼ cups all-purpose flour
1 package (8 ounces) almond paste
2 eggs
30 candied red cherries

CHOCOLATE GLAZE

½ cup semisweet chocolate morsels
1 teaspoon butter

Preheat the oven to 350 degrees. Lightly grease a 9 by 13-inch baking pan.

In a mixing bowl beat ½ cup of butter until creamy. Add ½ cup of sugar and continue beating until well blended. Beat in the vanilla and salt. Gradually add the flour and mix well. Gather mixture together, then pat the dough into the baking pan ①. Bake for 12 to 15 minutes, then cool slightly.

In a bowl, beat the almond paste, remaining sugar, and remaining butter until well blended. Beat in the eggs, 1 at a time, mixing well after each. Spread this mixture on top of the baked bottom layer. Arrange the cherries on top, spacing them in 6 rows of 5 cherries each ②. Bake an additional 20 to 25 minutes, or until the top layer springs back when touched.

Make the glaze by melting the chocolate and butter over hot (*not* boiling) water. Beat until well combined, then drizzle the glaze over the cooked pastry ③. When glaze has set, cut into 30 pieces with a cherry in the center of each.

YIELD

3 dozen

Per cookie
calories 70, protein 1 g, fat 4 g,
sodium 29 mg, carbohydrates
8 g, potassium 33 mg

TIME

15 minutes preparation
25 minutes baking

INGREDIENTS

1/2 cup butter, softened
1/4 cup firmly packed dark brown
   sugar
1 egg, separated
1 cup all-purpose flour
1 cup finely chopped unsalted peanuts
1/2 cup grape jelly

Preheat the oven to 300 degrees. Lightly grease a cookie sheet.

In a medium bowl cream the butter and brown sugar until light and fluffy. Add the egg yolk, then the flour and beat until well blended.

Lightly beat the egg white. Using a rounded 1/2 teaspoon measure of dough, form balls of dough ①. Dip each ball into the egg white and then into the chopped peanuts ②.

Place the balls on the cookie sheet and, using your fingertip, make a small depression in each one ③. Bake for 5 minutes, then remove the cookie sheet from the oven and press the centers again. Return cookies to oven and bake for an additional 20 minutes. Cool completely and fill centers with grape jelly.

YIELD

5 dozen

Per cookie
calories 71, protein 1 g, fat 3 g, sodium 52 mg, carbohydrates 10 g, potassium 25 mg

TIME

15 minutes preparation
3 to 4 hours chilling
8 to 10 minutes baking

INGREDIENTS

½ cup plus 1 tablespoon butter
6 tablespoons cocoa
1⅔ cups granulated sugar
2 eggs
2 teaspoons vanilla extract
2 cups all-purpose flour
½ teaspoon salt
2 teaspoons baking powder
1 cup coarsely chopped walnuts
Confectioners' sugar

Preheat the oven to 350 degrees.

Melt the butter and stir in the cocoa; blend well, then cool. Add the sugar, eggs, and vanilla, and beat until smooth.

In a separate bowl sift together the flour, salt, and baking powder. Add to the cocoa mixture ①, then add the walnuts. Chill for at least 3 hours.

Take 1 teaspoon of dough and shape it into a ball ②. Use the rest of the dough to make the remaining balls. Roll balls in confectioners' sugar ③, then place on an ungreased cookie sheet and bake for 8 to 10 minutes. Remove from oven as soon as they are set; the centers should be moist. Cool.

NOTE Cookies should be soft and chewy inside like a brownie.

PRUNE-WALNUT BREAD

YIELD

1 loaf, about 12 slices

Per slice
calories 283, protein 5 g,
fat 14 g, sodium 157 mg,
carbohydrates 36 g, potassium
214 mg

TIME

15 minutes preparation
50 to 60 minutes baking

INGREDIENTS

1½ cups all-purpose flour
⅔ cup granulated sugar
½ cup wheat germ
1¼ teaspoons apple pie spice
1 teaspoon baking soda
¼ teaspoon salt
½ cup butter, cut into chunks
2 eggs
½ cup sour cream
1 cup diced pitted prunes
½ cup chopped walnuts

Preheat the oven to 375 degrees. Lightly grease an 8½-by-4-inch baking pan or loaf pan.

In a large bowl combine the flour, sugar, wheat germ, apple pie spice, baking soda, and salt. Add the butter and, using a pastry blender, 2 knives, or your fingers, cut in until the mixture resembles coarse meal ①.

In a small bowl combine the eggs and sour cream. Blend into the flour mixture ②, then stir in the prunes and walnuts until just mixed. Spoon the batter into the baking pan ③ and bake for 50 to 60 minutes or until a cake tester comes out clean. Allow to cool in the pan for 10 minutes, then remove cake and cool completely on a rack. Serve warm or cooled with butter or cream cheese, if desired.

CANDY CANES

YIELD

1½ dozen

Per cookie
calories 184, protein 2 g,
fat 10 g, sodium 12 mg,
carbohydrates 20 g, potassium
12 mg

TIME

30 minutes preparation
1 hour chilling
9 to 10 minutes baking

INGREDIENTS

1 cup butter, softened
1 cup sifted confectioners' sugar
1 egg
2½ cups all-purpose flour
Dash of salt
¼ teaspoon vanilla extract
¼ teaspoon peppermint flavoring
Red food coloring or food paste
Red cinnamon candies
Green paper holly leaves

Cream the butter and sugar until light and fluffy. Beat in egg.

Combine flour and salt on a sheet of wax paper, then add to the creamed mixture and blend.

Divide the dough in half. Knead the vanilla into one half, and the peppermint flavoring and red food coloring into the other half. Chill both doughs for about 1 hour.

Preheat the oven to 350 degrees.

Break off a piece of peppermint dough and roll it into a rope about 8 inches long ①. Do the same with a piece of vanilla dough. Twist the peppermint and vanilla dough ropes together ②, and place on an ungreased cookie sheet. Curve the top to make a cane handle ③. Continue to make remaining cookie canes.

Bake canes for 9 to 10 minutes or until lightly browned; do not allow to become too brown. Decorate canes with red cinnamon candies and green paper holly leaves, if desired.

YIELD

12 to 16 servings

Per serving
calories 379, protein 5 g,
fat 21 g, sodium 141 mg,
carbohydrates 46 g, potassium
139 mg

TIME

20 minutes preparation
35 to 40 minutes baking

INGREDIENTS

½ cup sifted cocoa, plus additional
    for dusting
1 teaspoon baking soda
½ cup boiling water
½ cup butter
1¾ cups granulated sugar
2 eggs
1½ teaspoons vanilla extract
1½ cups all-purpose flour

1 cup buttermilk
1½ cups heavy cream
2 tablespoons confectioners' sugar
Chocolate curls or other decoration

Preheat oven to 350 degrees. Lightly grease a 13-by-9-by-2-inch baking pan, then dust with sifted cocoa.

In a small bowl combine the ½ cup cocoa, baking soda, and boiling water. Mix well and set aside.

In a large mixer bowl, cream the butter and sugar until light and fluffy ①. Add the eggs, 1 at a time, beating well after each. Stir in 1 teaspoon of vanilla.

Add the flour to the creamed mixture, alternating with the buttermilk and beginning and ending with the flour ②. Stir in cocoa mixture and blend well. Pour the mixture into the baking pan ③ and bake for 35 to 40 minutes or until a cake tester comes out clean. Cool completely.

Beat the cream until soft, then add confectioners' sugar and remaining vanilla. Continue to beat until soft peaks form. Spread cream over cake and garnish with chocolate curls or another decoration.

YIELD

3 dozen

Per cookie

calories 75, protein 1 g, fat 6 g, sodium 38 mg, carbohydrates 5 g, potassium 18 mg

TIME

15 minutes preparation
20 minutes cooking

INGREDIENTS

2 eggs
3 tablespoons granulated sugar
½ teaspoon salt
2 tablespoons vegetable oil
½ cup evaporated milk
½ cup water
1 cup all-purpose flour
Vegetable shortening for deep-frying
Confectioners' sugar

Whisk together the eggs and sugar. Beat in the salt, oil, evaporated milk, water, and flour. Mixture should be smooth.

Heat the shortening to 400 degrees. Dip the rosette iron into the oil and get it hot. Drain excess oil onto paper towels.

Dip the hot iron into the batter ①, just until top of the form. (If you go over the top, the rosette will not fall off as it cooks.) Fry until golden brown ②. Turn once. Remove cookie with a 2-pronged fork ③, and drain well on paper towels. Dip iron into hot oil before dipping into batter again; repeat for each rosette. Sprinkle rosettes with confectioners' sugar. Serve warm or cool.

CHOCOLATE ALMOND SNACKS

YIELD

about 2 dozen

Per cookie
calories 106, protein 1 g,
fat 7 g, sodium 42 mg,
carbohydrates 10 g, potassium
58 mg

TIME

10 minutes preparation
15 minutes baking

INGREDIENTS

1/2 cup plus 1 teaspoon butter
1/2 cup firmly packed brown sugar
1 egg yolk
1 teaspoon vanilla extract
1/2 cup all-purpose flour
1/2 cup quick-cooking rolled oats
1/2 cup semisweet chocolate morsels
1/2 cup sliced almonds

Preheat the oven to 375 degrees. Grease a 9 by 13-inch baking pan.

In a large bowl cream 1/2 cup of the butter and the sugar. Add the egg yolk and vanilla and stir well. Stir in the flour and oats and combine well.

Press the batter evenly into a thin layer on the bottom of the baking pan ①. Bake for 15 minutes, then cool slightly.

Melt the chocolate morsels and remaining butter over hot (*not* boiling) water. Spread the chocolate over the warm cookie crust ②. Sprinkle with the sliced almonds and press them in slightly with the back of a spoon ③. While still warm, cut into sections. Cool completely before removing from pan.

NUT TASSIES

YIELD

2 dozen

Per pastry
calories 121, protein 2 g,
fat 8 g, sodium 71 mg,
carbohydrates 11 g, potassium
53 mg

TIME

30 minutes preparation
2 hours chilling
25 minutes baking

INGREDIENTS

1 package (3 ounces) cream cheese
½ cup plus 1 tablespoon butter,
   softened
1 cup all-purpose flour
1 egg
¾ cup firmly packed brown sugar
1 teaspoon vanilla extract
⅛ teaspoon salt
⅔ cup finely chopped nuts

In a medium bowl cream the cream cheese with ½ cup of the butter. Stir in the flour. Gather into a ball and wrap securely and chill for 2 hours.

Preheat the oven to 325 degrees.

Divide the dough into 24 1-inch balls and press each one onto the sides and bottom of ungreased 1½-inch muffin cups ①.

Melt the remaining tablespoon of butter, then beat with the egg and sugar. Add the vanilla and salt.

Sprinkle one third of the nuts onto the dough-lined muffin cups ②. Cover the nuts evenly with the egg-sugar mixture ③. Sprinkle with the remaining nuts and bake for 20 minutes. Raise the temperature to 375 degrees, and bake 5 minutes longer. Cool slightly, then remove from the muffin cups and cool completely on a rack.

28

YIELD

9 filled cookies

Per cookie
calories 335, protein 5 g,
fat 15 g, sodium 114 mg,
carbohydrates 48 g, potassium
113 mg

TIME

20 minutes preparation
4 to 5 hours chilling
8 to 10 minutes baking

INGREDIENTS

1½ cups all-purpose flour
1 tablespoon sifted cocoa
1 teaspoon ground cinnamon
¾ cup granulated sugar
½ cup ground shelled almonds
½ cup butter, cut into pieces
1 egg
½ cup raspberry or apricot jam
Confectioners' sugar

In a medium bowl combine the flour, cocoa, cinnamon, sugar, and almonds. Toss lightly with a fork, add the butter pieces, and cut in with a pastry blender or use your fingertips. Stir in the egg and mix completely. Gather into a ball. Wrap securely in plastic wrap and chill for 4 to 5 hours.

Preheat the oven to 350 degrees.

On a lightly floured surface roll out half the dough until ¼ inch thick. Cut out rounds using a 3-inch biscuit cutter. With the remaining half of the dough cut out rounds with the same cutter, but cut a smaller circle (about ¾ inch) in the center ①, using a bottle cap.

Place both batches on an ungreased cookie sheet and bake for 8 to 10 minutes. Remove from the cookie sheet and cool completely.

Spread the plain cookies with raspberry or apricot jam ② and cover with a cookie with a hole in the center ③. Sprinkle tops with confectioners' sugar.

CHINESE ALMOND COOKIES

YIELD

2 dozen

Per cookie
calories 171, protein 2 g,
fat 11 g, sodium 53 mg,
carbohydrates 16 g, potassium
30 mg

TIME

15 minutes preparation
2 to 3 hours chilling
15 minutes baking

INGREDIENTS

1 cup lard
2 eggs
3/4 cup granulated sugar
1 tablespoon almond extract
2 1/4 cups all-purpose flour
1 teaspoon baking powder
1/2 teaspoon baking soda
1/4 teaspoon salt

GLAZE/DECORATION

1 egg, slightly beaten
24 blanched almonds

Cream together in a medium bowl the lard, eggs, sugar, and almond extract. Combine flour, baking powder, baking soda, and salt in a mixing bowl and toss gently with a fork. Combine the dry mixture with the creamed mixture and blend well.

Divide dough into 2 portions and form each into a cylinder approximately 1 1/2 inches in diameter. Wrap securely in plastic wrap and refrigerate for 2 to 3 hours.

Preheat the oven to 400 degrees. Cut 12 equal slices from each roll and place on an ungreased cookie sheet, leaving about 1 inch between the slices. Brush slices with beaten egg and press a whole almond firmly into the center of each. Bake for 15 minutes or until slightly brown around the edges. Cool on a rack.

SPRITZ COOKIES

YIELD

5 dozen

Per cookie
calories 55, protein 1 g, fat 3 g,
sodium 7 mg, carbohydrates
6 g, potassium 7 mg

TIME

15 minutes preparation
10 to 12 minutes baking

INGREDIENTS

1 cup butter, softened
3/4 cup granulated sugar
1 egg
2 1/4 cups all-purpose flour
1/2 teaspoon baking powder
Dash of salt
1 teaspoon almond, vanilla, or lemon
   extract
Decorations for cookies (optional)

Preheat the oven to 400 degrees.

Cream together the butter and sugar until light and fluffy. Add the egg and mix well. In a separate bowl combine the flour, baking powder, and salt. Combine dry mixture with the creamed mixture and stir in the flavoring.

Using about one-fourth of the dough at a time, place a portion into a cookie press using a star disc or other shape. Press cookies out onto the cookie sheet, leaving about 2 inches between. Decorate with sprinkles, jimmies, candied cherries, or nut halves. Bake for 8 to 10 minutes, or until just beginning to brown, then remove to rack to cool.

RASPBERRY-NUT SHORTBREAD BARS

YIELD

18 bars

Per cookie
calories 194, protein 3 g, fat 10 g, sodium 80 mg, carbohydrates 24 g, potassium 75 mg

TIME

15 minutes preparation
42 to 45 minutes baking

INGREDIENTS

1 1/4 cups all-purpose flour
1/2 cup granulated sugar
1/2 cup butter
1/3 cup raspberry jam

TOPPING

2 large eggs
1/2 cup firmly packed brown sugar
1 teaspoon vanilla extract
2 tablespoons all-purpose flour
1/8 teaspoon salt
1/8 teaspoon baking soda
1 cup chopped nuts

Preheat the oven to 350 degrees. Lightly grease a 9-inch square baking pan.

In a medium bowl combine the flour, sugar, and butter. Mix with your fingertips until the mixture is like fine meal. Press mixture over the bottom of the baking pan to make an even layer.

Bake shortbread layer for 20 minutes, just until the edges become tinged with brown. Remove from the oven and spread raspberry jam over the shortbread.

Beat the eggs with the brown sugar and vanilla until well blended. Stir in the flour, salt, and soda and then stir in the nuts. Pour over the jam layer and return cookies to the oven. Bake for 22 to 25 minutes longer, or until topping has set. Cool in the pan, then cut into bars.

AUNT KITTY'S NUT PUFFS

YIELD

5 dozen

Per cookie
calories 58, protein 1 g, fat 4 g, sodium .5 mg, carbohydrates 4 g, potassium 14 mg

TIME

10 minutes preparation
2 to 3 hours chilling
10 to 12 minutes baking

INGREDIENTS

1 cup butter, softened
3 tablespoons confectioners' sugar
1 teaspoon vanilla extract
2 teaspoons water
2 cups all-purpose flour
1 cup chopped walnuts
Confectioners' sugar for rolling

In a mixing bowl cream the butter and sugar. Add the vanilla and water and mix well. Add the flour and nuts and mix well. Cover with plastic wrap and chill for 2 to 3 hours.

Preheat the oven to 400 degrees. Take tablespoon-size bits of the dough and roll into 1-inch balls. Place the dough balls on an ungreased cookie sheet and bake for 10 to 12 minutes.

Fill a small plastic bag with confectioners' sugar. While the nut puffs are still warm, place a few at a time into the bag and shake well until they are covered with sugar. Roll again in sugar when completely cooled.

Index